**NATIONAL
GEOGRAPHIC**

D1466092

JAMESTOWN

and the Virginia Colony

Daniel Rosen

PICTURE CREDITS
Cover, 2-3, 3 (border), 6 (border), 15 (border), 16, 19, 21 (top, bottom, and border), 26 (right), 27, 28, 29 (left and right), 31 (bottom and border), 34, (bottom), 38, 39 (border), 40 (border) The Granger Collection, NY; cover (inset), 24-25, 37 Colonial Williamsburg Foundation; page 1 Giraudon/Art Resource, NY; pages 4-5, 33 (left) Bettmann/Corbis; page 4 Dave G. Houser/Corbis; page 6 Tate Gallery, London/Art Resource, NY; page 7 Richard T. Nowitz/Corbis; page 8 The British Museum; pages 9, 12, 14, 15, 23 National Park Service, Colonial National Historic Park; pages 10 (top), 11 Stock Montage; page 10 (bottom) Art Resource, NY; page 17 Jamestown-Yorktown Educational Trust; page 18 National Portrait Gallery, Smithsonian Institution/Art Resource, NY; page 18 (frame) Photodisc/Getty Images; page 26 (left) Adam Woolfitt/Corbis; page 30 N. Carter/North Wind Picture Library; page 32 Library of Virginia; page 33 (right) Gianni Dagli Orti/Corbis; page 35 National Maritime Museum, Greenwich, UK; page 36 (top) George H. H. Huey/Corbis.

QUOTATIONS
page 4 George Percy from "Observations Gathered out of 'A Discourse of the Plantation of the Southern Colony in Virginia by the English'" (1606); page 8 John Smith from A True Relation (1607); page 11 John Smith from The Generall Historie (1624); page 17 John Rolfe from a letter to Sir Thomas Dale, governor of Virginia (1614); page 20 Edward Waterhouse from "A Declaration of the State of the Colony and . . . a Relation of the Barbarous massacre" (1622); page 26 from a Virginia Slave Code (1680); page 32 John Pory, from "A Report of the General Assembly" (1619); page 36 Nathaniel Bacon, from "The Declaration of the People Against Sir William Berkeley" (1676).

Produced through the worldwide resources of the National Geographic Society, John M. Fahey, Jr., President and Chief Executive Officer; Gilbert M. Grosvenor, Chairman of the Board; Nina D. Hoffman, Executive Vice President and President, Books and Education Publishing Group.

PREPARED BY NATIONAL GEOGRAPHIC SCHOOL PUBLISHING
Ericka Markman, Senior Vice President and President, Children's Books and Education Publishing Group; Steve Mico, Vice President, Editorial Director; Marianne Hiland, Executive Editor; Anita Schwartz, Project Editor, Jim Hiscott, Design Manager; Kristin Hanneman, Illustrations Manager; Diana Bourdrez, Picture Editor; Matt Wascavage, Manager of Publishing Services; Sean Philpotts, Production Manager.

MANUFACTURING AND QUALITY MANAGEMENT
Christopher A. Liedel, Chief Financial Officer; Phillip L. Schlosser, Director; Clifton M. Brown, Manager.

PROGRAM DEVELOPMENT
Gare Thompson Associates, Inc.

CONSULTANTS/REVIEWERS
Dr. Margit E. McGuire, School of Education, Seattle University, Seattle, Washington

BOOK DEVELOPMENT
Nieman, Inc.

BOOK DESIGN
Three Communication Design, LLC

ART DIRECTOR
Dan Banks, Project Design Company

MAP DEVELOPMENT AND PRODUCTION
Bruce Burdick

Published by the National Geographic Society
Washington, D.C. 20036-4688

Product No. 4J41741

ISBN-13: 978-0-7922-4547-6
ISBN-10: 0-7922-4547-4

Printed in Canada

11 10 09 08
10 9 8 7 6

TABLE OF CONTENTS

These houses in the Colonial National Historical Park at Jamestown have been made to look like the original ones.

"*April 26th we first saw the coast of Virginia. We entered Chesapeake Bay and landed, discovering fair meadows and goodly tall trees with such fresh waters running through the woods, I was stunned at the sight.*"

–GEORGE PERCY, Jamestown colonist

4

Introduction

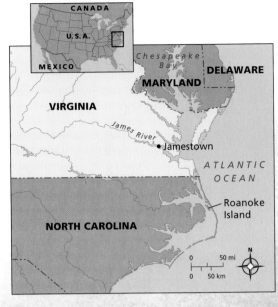

Why would people leave their homes and families to risk an ocean journey of more than 3,000 miles? Why would they give up the comforts of a settled life for the unknown dangers of a new land?

England in the late 1500s was not a pleasant place for most people. Many people were out of work. Many had lost their homes. Some saw a chance for a better life in America. They hoped to ship furs, fish, and timber back to England to make their fortune. Others believed that they would find gold and silver in America. Still others wanted to farm.

People like these were among the first small groups of English settlers who sailed to the new land. They arrived in what is now the state of Virginia. The Virginia **Colony** became the first permanent English settlement in America. In the earliest years of the Virginia Colony, the Virginians made some decisions that would shape the history of America.

The earliest English settlers were taking the first step on the road to building the modern United States. Many brave people followed them. This is their story.

Chapter 1

Starting Jamestown

Virginia's story begins with a disaster. In 1587, English colonists settled on an island they called Roanoke. The island is off the coast of present-day North Carolina. The Roanoke Colony did not last. When leaders returned with supplies from England in 1590, everyone had disappeared.

The fate of the Lost Colony, as it was called, is still a mystery. This disaster stopped the English from returning to Virginia for a short time. After a while, the idea of riches won out over any fear of what might happen.

In 1606, a group of London businessmen decided they could get rich in North America. They formed a company called the Virginia Company. They asked King James I of England for a charter, or a permit, to start a colony in Virginia. The charter stated the rights, duties, and goals of the company. The king thought a colony would benefit England. He granted the charter.

Three ships left London for Virginia in December 1606. The ships carried about 100 colonists and all the things they would need. Who were these brave people? They were all men. Some of them were farmers. Others were servants. A few were skilled craftsmen. Many of them were gentlemen. At that time in England, gentlemen did not do physical labor. These men did not expect to do any work in the Virginia Colony either.

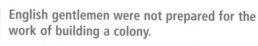
English gentlemen were not prepared for the work of building a colony.

ARRIVAL IN VIRGINIA

The English had learned something from earlier failures, but they hadn't learned enough. They sent people to the new land who had no skills or desire to work. They were not planning to clear forests and plant crops. They believed their only work would be bending over to pick up all the gold and silver on the ground. They were going to the Virginia Colony to strike it rich.

Crossing the Atlantic had left most of the travelers seasick and weak. They wondered if they had made the right choice. Then, on April 26, 1607, they first saw the coast of Virginia. The beauty of the land stunned them. Flowers were in bloom. Dense forests with wild game covered the land. The settlers saw Virginia as a land of opportunity.

For the next few weeks, the colonists explored the coast. They sailed up a river they named the James. On May 14, they chose a place for their settlement. They called it Jamestown. Both the river and the town were named in honor of England's King James I.

These are copies of two of the three Jamestown ships, the *Susan Constant* (left) and the *Godspeed* (right).

The Colonists and the Native Americans

The Native Americans who lived in the area were the Powhatan (pow-uh-TAN). They were a tall, dignified people. They farmed, fished, and hunted. They had a powerful chief, also called Powhatan. He led some nine thousand people. The Powhatan men were **warriors**. They thought of war as a kind of deadly sport. Men went to war to show their courage. Raids on enemy villages were common. So, the settlers' first task was to build a log fort.

Tattooed Powhatan warrior with bow

Relations between the Indians and the settlers were always uneasy. To the Powhatan, the colonists were **invaders**. The English thought they were bringing **civilization** to the Indians. They believed that the English way of life was the best way.

Yet, the settlers needed Powhatan help. They traded with the Indians for food. The Powhatan were glad to trade for metal tools and guns. They didn't know how to make such things. But they had little food to trade. They grew only enough food to last into early spring. The settlers' demands put the tribe at risk. If they gave the settlers too much food, they themselves could starve. The differences between the Indians and colonists would cause trouble between the two groups.

Voices from America

"In our great need, the Indians brought us corn when we rather expected they would destroy us."

–JOHN SMITH, leader of the Virginia Colony

8

THE FIRST MONTHS

Soon, problems developed. The place the colonists chose for their settlement proved to be a mistake. They had chosen land that stuck out into the river. They thought that this made good sense. The deep water let the colonists tie their ships up close to land. But the land was **marshy**. The soil was poor. Salt water backed up from the ocean and got into the drinking water. Mosquitoes thrived in the marshy land. The mosquitoes spread malaria. This disease killed many settlers.

Many colonists became ill from drinking the bad water. The few crops the men had planted were not yet ripe. They were low on supplies. The settlers grew weak from lack of food. They were often unable to hunt or fish because of the danger of attack by the Native Americans. Life in Jamestown did not get off to a good start. These early months were hard.

Settlers gathering logs to build a fence around the fort

9

A LEADER SAVES THE COLONY

All through that first summer, people died. By September, more than half the settlers were dead. The leaders argued among themselves. No one could decide what to do. Would Jamestown suffer the same fate as the Lost Colony? The settlers needed a leader, or they would all die.

Captain John Smith

At last, one man took charge. His name was Captain John Smith. Smith was 27 years old when he arrived in Jamestown. As a soldier he already had lived through enough adventures for a man twice his age. He knew how to survive in the wilderness. He knew that the settlers had to work and farm, not search for gold.

Smith gave orders for each man to work on building the fort and gathering food. When the gentlemen reminded Smith of their rank, Smith had a simple answer: "He who will not work, will not eat." The gentlemen went to work. Smith helped the settlers survive.

Powhatan village

Pocahontas pleading with her father to save John Smith's life

JOHN SMITH AND POCAHONTAS

In December 1607, Smith almost died when the Indians captured him. They took him to the chief. Smith later wrote a book about his experiences. When the warriors picked up their clubs and rocks, he was certain he was about to die. According to Smith, just before they came at him, Pocahontas, Powhatan's 13-year-old daughter, rushed out. She laid her head across Smith's body.

In Smith's account, the chief was moved by his daughter's actions. Instead of killing him, they adopted Smith into the tribe. He returned to Jamestown with not only his life. He had also won the friendship of the chief.

Pocahontas did more than save John Smith's life. Over the next few years, she helped save the colony. She brought food to the colonists. She also helped the newcomers trade for goods with her people. She warned the settlers about raids the Powhatan planned against them. They were able to prepare themselves for battle because of her early warnings.

A Deadly Time

The Powhatan released Smith in January 1608. When he returned to Jamestown, he found a group of cold and hungry settlers. Smith was a great leader, but the colony still faced many challenges.

Remarkably, on the same day he returned, a ship from England sailed up the river. It carried about 100 new settlers, along with food and supplies. The colony's bad luck continued, however. A few days later, a fire broke out in the village, destroying most of it.

Soon after new settlers arrived, a fire burned houses inside the walls of the fort.

While the settlers rebuilt their village, Smith went back to the Powhatan to trade for food. The Native Americans and the settlers also exchanged hostages as a way of keeping the peace. Still, the weakened settlers continued to die. By spring, only 38 were left. Most had died of starvation or illness.

Meet | Tom Savage

Tom Savage was a 13-year-old orphan in England. In 1608, he talked his way onto Captain Newport's ship that was sailing for Jamestown. The captain liked the boy. He took him on as an **indentured servant**. That meant Tom would have to work for Newport for seven years to pay for his passage to America.

In Jamestown, Tom expected to work as a field hand for Newport. Then, Captain Newport and John Smith discovered that Native American tribes sometimes traded children. So, the colonists exchanged Tom for an Indian boy named Namontack.

Tom lived with the Powhatan for three years. He learned their language and their customs. Tom became a spy for the colonists. He told them when the Powhatan planned attacks. As a reward, Newport freed Tom from his indenture.

TROUBLE AHEAD

In the fall of 1608, another ship arrived with more settlers, including the first two women. Bad luck continued. Rats had eaten most of the ship's supplies for the settlers. Smith organized fishing and hunting parties. He made sure everyone worked hard to get food. As a result, very few settlers died that winter.

In 1609, John Smith was badly hurt. By accident, his bag carrying his gunpowder exploded. He sailed back to England to get treatment for his injuries. Before leaving Jamestown, Smith looked over the storehouses. He was pleased to see that the colony had enough food to get through the winter.

The future of Jamestown looked brighter. There were now about 500 colonists. Among the new colonists was a woman named Anne Burras. She married settler John Laydon. It was the first wedding in Jamestown.

Smith planned to return to Jamestown. Although he returned to America, he never made it back to Jamestown. However, he wrote a book that told of life there. His book inspired many people to come to North America. Smith thought that he had left a colony that would have no trouble surviving.

More women arrived in Jamestown after 1609.

THE STARVING TIME

Colonists carry the dead away for burial.

When John Smith left Jamestown, there were 500 settlers. By the spring of 1610, only 60 were still alive. What could have happened in such a short time? How did the settlers die?

The Powhatan had become more and more angry with the settlers for taking their land. With Smith gone, they decided to try to wipe out the colony. They would starve the colonists.

They killed off the wild game around Jamestown that the colonists hunted for meat. Then they surrounded the village. The colonists could not leave to hunt or fish. Quickly they went through their storehouse of food. Then they ate their cattle and goats. Next they ate their dogs and finally rats and mice.

The colonists starved and died through that long, terrible winter. By spring, the few who were left were ready to leave the colony. Jamestown seemed to be finished at last. The colonists called the winter of 1609–1610 the Starving Time.

A New Beginning

In late spring of 1610, a single ship sailed into Jamestown harbor. The passengers and crew were shocked by what they found. The few remaining settlers were eager to leave. They packed up the little of value they had and climbed aboard the ship, ready to return to England. Was this finally the end of Jamestown?

As the ship began to sail down the James River, three more English ships appeared. They were bringing more colonists, some soldiers, and food and supplies to the colony. The new governor, Lord Thomas De la Warr (for whom the state of Delaware is named), was aboard. He ordered the fleeing colonists to turn around and go back to Jamestown.

De la Warr took charge of the colony. He set out to change the way the colony was run. He put the new settlers to work immediately. The colony now tried harder to get along with the Powhatan. For several years the two groups were able to live together in peace. Jamestown would survive. But how would the settlers earn money?

Royal governor Lord De la Warr arrives in Jamestown.

15

BROWN GOLD

By now everyone knew that no gold or silver was to be found in the Virginia Colony. The colonists needed to find some other way to make money. One of the settlers, John Rolfe, had an idea. Smoking tobacco had become popular in Europe.

Tobacco grew wild in the Virginia Colony, but it tasted harsh and bitter. Rolfe began experimenting with tobacco plants. After many tries, Rolfe grew a plant that had a sweet taste. In 1614, he sent the first of the new tobacco to England. The people loved it. Jamestown had a future! By 1616, the colony was sending more than 2,000 pounds of tobacco to Europe.

Everyone rushed to grow tobacco. Many colonists stopped growing food crops to plant all their land with tobacco. They even planted it along the streets of the town. The governor insisted that every colonist grow at least some corn. Otherwise, the colony would go hungry. At last the colonists had a way to make money. For the first time they were working hard. Maybe the colony would make it after all.

Tobacco farming made the colony profitable.

JOHN ROLFE AND POCAHONTAS

Because of tobacco, John Rolfe became one of the most famous colonists. He is also remembered for another reason. He married Pocahontas, daughter of the Powhatan chief.

One day, Pocahontas was visiting friends when the settlers kidnapped her. The Powhatan and the settlers were not getting along. The colonists hoped to trade Pocahontas for peace with the Indians.

John Rolfe experimented with his tobacco plants.

Chief Powhatan did not reply to this offer for three months. During this time, the colonists treated Pocahontas well. She learned English. She learned the manners of a "proper" Englishwoman. She became a Christian and was given the name of Rebecca. She felt at home with the settlers.

Pocahontas met the tobacco planter, John Rolfe. The two fell in love. Rolfe wrote a letter to the governor asking to marry her. Pocahontas also asked Powhatan. Both men agreed. The wedding was held in April 1614, in the church in Jamestown. Pocahontas' father did not come. But her uncle, an important chief, came for the ceremony.

Voices from America

"It is Pocahontas, to whom my hearty and best thoughts are, and have been a long time. . . ."

—JOHN ROLFE, in a letter to the governor

THE PEACE OF POCAHONTAS

Rolfe and Pocahontas had a baby boy, Thomas. The young family went to England on a visit. They went to attract new settlers to the colony and to help tobacco sales. People became very interested in Pocahontas. She was known as Lady Rebecca. King James I and Queen Anne received her. She had her portrait painted. Pocahontas became popular in London society.

While in England, Pocahontas became ill. Just as the young family was ready to return to Virginia in 1617, Pocahontas died. She was only 22. John Rolfe, alone and sad, returned to Virginia. Thomas stayed with relatives in England and went to school there. When he was a young man, Thomas returned to Virginia.

Pocahontas dressed in English clothes

MASSACRE

Pocahontas and John Rolfe's marriage helped keep the peace for a while. Chief Powhatan made sure of that. Then in 1618, Powhatan died. His brother became the new leader of the Powhatan people. This new leader did not like or trust the English. He planned to get rid of the settlers once and for all. He took his time to prepare. He wanted to take the settlers by surprise.

After years of peace, the colonists felt safe. They stopped carrying guns everywhere. They traded with the Indians. Peace seemed to rule the day. Then in March 1622, the Powhatan chief led a group to Jamestown. They came to trade furs and corn for English goods. At least that is what the settlers thought. Suddenly, the Native Americans turned on the settlers. They killed about 350 colonists, roughly a third of the total. One of them was John Rolfe.

The Powhatan attack ▶

THE NATIVE AMERICANS ARE DEFEATED

The massacre of 1622 was another setback for Jamestown. It also marked the beginning of the end for the Native Americans. The colonists armed themselves. They started regular attacks on the Indians. They destroyed crops and burned Indian villages. Native Americans' arrows were no match for English guns, and many Indians were killed. They learned that the colonists could not be beaten.

After the massacre, the colonists began to attack the Indians.

Voices from America

"We may now by right of war and law of nations invade the country and destroy them who sought to destroy us."

–EDWARD WATERHOUSE, a settler

The Virginia Colony Grows

Few people in England wanted to move to the Virginia Colony in its very early years. They had heard of the sickness, the unfriendly Indians, and the starvation. However, as time passed, they saw how successful growing tobacco was. Settlers were becoming rich. Also, the danger of Indian attack was fading.

Leaders of the colony wanted more settlers. So, they offered 50 acres of land in the colony to anyone who would pay for the trip. And for each additional person you brought, you got another 50 acres. A person with some money could quickly put together a large piece of land. For many, this was a great opportunity.

The Virginia Colony began to attract more settlers. In 1619, more than 1,000 settlers came to Virginia. Another 3,500 people arrived over the next three years. Many were hardworking people. Some were beggars. Others were teenaged orphans. All of them hoped to make a better life for themselves.

INDENTURED SERVANTS

Most settlers could not afford to pay for their passage to the new land. So, they became indentured servants. This meant they agreed to work for someone for a period of time, usually four to seven years. In return, they received passage from England and food, clothing, and shelter.

When their term of work ended, they were free to work for wages. Many of them saved their money. In time, they were able to buy small farms. By the mid-1600s, as many as three-quarters of all landowners in the Virginia Colony were former indentured servants.

Indentured servants were not slaves. But their lives were often not that different from the lives of slaves. They had to work long hours. Sometimes they barely got enough to eat. They could be whipped. One thing was different, of course. In time, they would be free. Often, however, they didn't live long enough to complete their term of work. Many newcomers died from disease, the harsh climate, and hard work.

Ships brought workers to the colony and returned to England with tobacco.

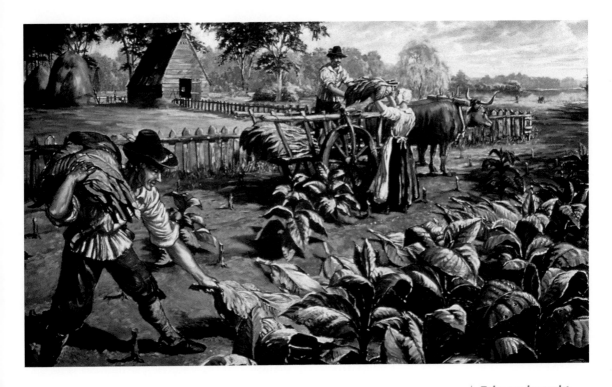

GROWING TOBACCO

The Virginia Colony was an ideal place for growing tobacco.
There was plenty of rich land. Many rivers flowed through it
to the sea. Wealthy planters built **plantations**, or large farms,
along these rivers. The more tobacco they grew, the wealthier
they became.

Growing tobacco wore out the soil. Each year the crop was not
as good as the one the year before. After about seven years,
planters could not farm the same land anymore. There was a
simple solution to this problem. Land was cheap. So, planters
bought more land. They cleared it and grew tobacco.

New farmland needed more workers. Workers were becoming
harder to find. Many indentured servants had already won their
freedom. They now had their own farms to work. Life in England
was better. Fewer new workers were coming to the colony. Who
would work these new plantations? Slaves would.

23

SLAVERY ARRIVES IN VIRGINIA

The first captured Africans came to the Virginia Colony in 1619. A Dutch ship arrived carrying a cargo of Africans. The Africans had been sold to the Dutch captain. He then sold them to the Jamestown planters. Planters desperately needed help growing and harvesting tobacco.

The planters were unsure how to treat these Africans at first. They treated some as indentured servants. In time, these people were freed. Some masters freed their slaves in their wills. One former slave was able to earn enough money to buy his daughters out of slavery. Some freed Africans even owned property.

Earlier, the settlers had tried to use Native Americans as workers. Some of them had run away. Many died from the new diseases brought by the English. They did not know how to farm the way the English did. African workers knew how to farm. They were healthier than the Indians were. The Africans also had nowhere to run.

Dutch ships brought the first African slaves to America in 1619.

SLAVERY GROWS

Slavery grew slowly at first. Slaves were expensive. Also, many planters did not like the idea of slavery. In 1650, there were only about 300 black people in the Virginia Colony.

Around 1660, things changed. Planters now had money. They could afford slaves. Their need for workers kept increasing. The number of settlers arriving grew smaller each year. The planters needed slaves.

Two things happened that promoted slavery. Slavery became legal in the Virginia Colony. At the same time, the price of slaves dropped. By 1671, there were about 2,000 African slaves in the colony. Owning slaves had become a way of life.

OWNING SLAVES

Many slaves lived in small cabins like these and were controlled through fear and punishment.

As the number of slaves grew, life in the Virginia Colony changed. In time, black slaves greatly outnumbered whites in many places. Blacks did not like being slaves. They did not gain anything from their work. So, they had no reason to work hard. They had to be made to work. Most were treated badly. They ran away when they could. White people were often afraid of their slaves. They feared their slaves might rise up against them.

Most slave owners controlled their slaves through punishment. Beatings were common. Runaways could be killed on the spot by anyone. The government paid the owner back for his loss if a runaway was killed. Sometimes slaves were punished by being sold.

Voices from America

"No slave may go from his owner's plantation without a certificate, the punishment twenty lashes on the bare back. If any Negro absent himself from his master's service, he may be killed."

—A VIRGINIA SLAVE CODE, 1680

THE GROWTH OF PLANTATIONS

Wealthier planters grew more powerful as their plantations became larger and larger. A plantation owner was more like a businessman than a farmer. Many owned several plantations. They had to clothe and feed hundreds of people living on the plantations. They also managed the production of many goods, such as clothes, shoes, and candles.

Smaller planters worked hard. They were not able to compete with the large landholders, however. Their farms stayed small. In time, many were forced off their land. The large plantation owners bought up their farms.

Some plantation owners grew wealthy and built huge homes.

THE TOBACCO TRADE

Mount Vernon was the home of George Washington.

A large plantation was both a farm and a village. That means the landowner grew or made many of the things that were needed, such as bricks. Planters sold their tobacco directly to British merchants. Money rarely changed hands. Most plantations traded tobacco for goods from England.

Virginia Colony plantations were like little islands. Their most direct ties were to England. Most transportation was by boat. There were few roads. Ships from England called at every plantation on the river. The ships brought such goods as furniture, fancy clothing, books, and tea. First the goods were unloaded. Then workers loaded tobacco onto the ships for the return trip to England.

> ## MEET | *John Washington*
>
> John Washington arrived in the Virginia Colony in 1657. He was a sailor. Washington looked around and decided to stay. Within a few years, he had his first plantation and was building more. John Washington grew to be an important man in the colony. His **descendant**, George Washington, was the first president of the United States.

PLANTER FAMILY LIFE

Plantation owners and their families lived well. They wore fine clothes made in England. Boys were expected to work hard at their studies. Most were taught at home by private tutors. They studied Latin, Greek, and mathematics as well as reading and writing. Often, the son of a planter would go to England for more schooling or college. They were trained to fill the role played by their father.

Girls from the richest families were taught how to read but not always how to write. Most of their lessons were about how to be ladies. They were expected to marry the sons of other planters. They had to know how to oversee many parts of plantation life. They would manage education, entertaining, and the making of household goods.

The cover of this spelling book shows ▶ a teacher giving his student wisdom.

◀ | Some wealthy children had slaves.

SMALL FARMS

Life couldn't have been more different for small farmers. Farmers grew tobacco for money. They also had to grow their own food and raise livestock. Women and children also worked to keep the farm going. There was little time for schooling for most children. When tobacco prices were high, a good crop could mean a good year for small farmers. A poor crop or low prices meant hard times and empty stomachs.

Hardworking farmers could be successful. However, they needed to have some good luck. It was not unusual for a small farmer to have servants or a few slaves as his farm grew.

Most farmers served in the local **militia,** or military force. The men were prepared to do battle with any enemy. The planter with the most land in the area was usually the commander. Every year, after the tobacco was harvested, the militia would gather for training. The men did more than drill. They also shared good times.

Most families lived in small houses.

Governing the Virginia Colony

In the early years of the Virginia Colony, the **investors** in the Virginia Company tried to run it. However, it took months for messages to travel back and forth across the Atlantic. Also, the colonists didn't want to obey rules made so far away.

The settlers wanted a larger say in their government. So, a lawmaking **assembly**, or group, was set up in the colony. White male landowners elected representatives, or burgesses (BER-jihs-sees), to the assembly. Each of the little settlements outside of Jamestown chose two burgesses. For the first time, settlers could choose some of the people who governed them.

Virginia's first colonial assembly meets in Jamestown.

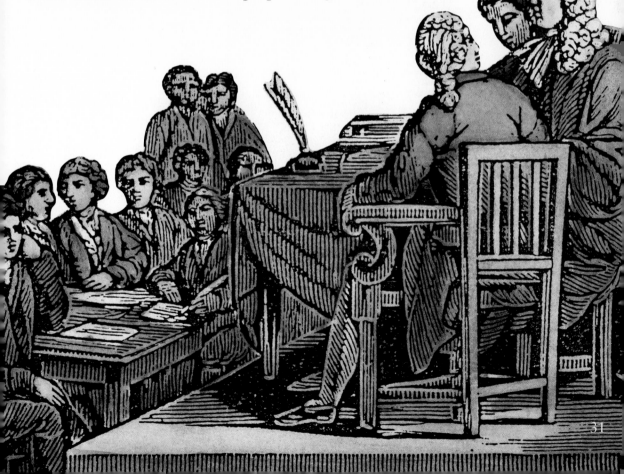

31

THE HOUSE OF BURGESSES

The new assembly was called the House of Burgesses. Its first meeting was held in Jamestown in the summer of 1619, the same year the first Africans arrived. It was the first meeting of an elected legislature in the English colonies. A legislature is a body of people that has the power to make laws.

This first meeting of the House of Burgesses lasted for just a few days. One of the first things it did was to give all settlers the rights of Englishmen. These rights included the right to liberty and to trial by jury. Another was the right to elect representatives to a governing body like the House of Burgesses.

The House of Burgesses was the first local government in colonial America.

The assembly usually met only once a year. The governor of the colony could veto, or turn down, any laws that the assembly passed. Even so, the House of Burgesses had real power. It could discuss any problems. It passed many laws. The House of Burgesses was the first step toward self-government in the land that was to become the United States. The people of the Virginia Colony began to feel that this new land really did belong to them.

Voices from America

"Do not take the laws we pass and our work lightly, for otherwise, the people will grow rebellious and become impossible to govern."

–JOHN PORY, member and secretary of the House of Burgesses, 1619. His record of the meetings of the assembly was sent to the Virginia Company.

The End of the Virginia Company

In 1624, the Virginia Company ran out of money. There were several reasons for its failure. The colonists insisted on over-production of tobacco. So, the company had to continue to help supply food to the colony. Because many settlers died over the years, the colony had not grown very much. Also, troubles with the Powhatan continued from time to time.

King James revoked, or canceled, the charter of the Virginia Company. Since the company could no longer appoint a governor, James appointed a royal governor.

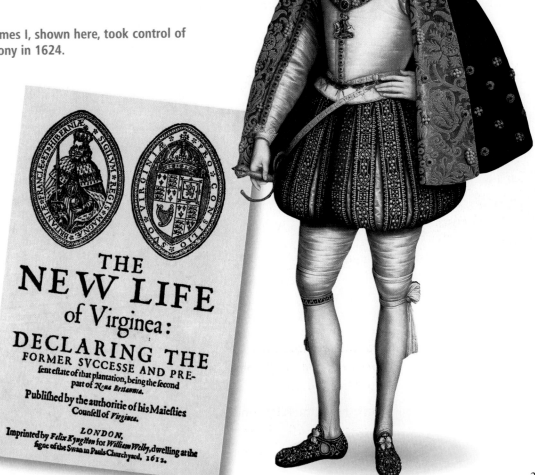

King James I, shown here, took control of the colony in 1624.

THE GENTRY

By the 1620s, the Virginia Colony had spread along the James River beyond Jamestown. The colony had representative government, but not all colonists could vote for their representatives. Only white men who owned land could vote. That meant only the wealthy planters, called the **gentry**, and small farmers could vote. Women and blacks could not vote.

Most government jobs were given to wealthy men. Many jobs were passed down from father to son. Although members of the House of Burgesses were elected, most of them also came from wealthy families. These men made and passed laws that protected the rights of the gentry. Because small farmers could vote, they kept some power. If a gentleman running for office did not agree to help the small farmers, they wouldn't vote for him.

Slaves work while their owner relaxes.

POLITICAL TROUBLES

In the 1660s and 1670s, things changed in Virginia. The price of tobacco fell sharply. Planters had grown too much tobacco. Wealthy planters and poor farmers alike were hurt.

Hard times led to political troubles. Governor William Berkeley and the planters in the House of Burgesses had become very close. Berkeley gave many special favors to the burgesses. In return, the burgesses supported him. Most of these favors benefited only the wealthy planters. The small farmers felt left out. No one was working to help them.

Native Americans were another problem. Berkeley said land in western Virginia was off-limits to settlers. He wanted to keep peace with the Indians. Poor farmers and freed indentured servants wanted land. The only open land was in the west. These settlers ignored the governor. They staked out farms in the west. They claimed the land. Soon, fights with the Indians broke out. The once peaceful and rich Virginia Colony was coming apart.

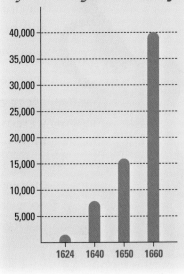

Population Growth of the Virginia Colony

MEET | *Governor Berkeley*

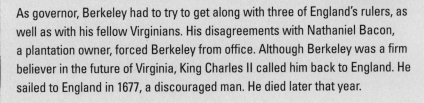

Born in England in 1606, William Berkeley was appointed governor of Virginia in 1641 by King Charles I. He arrived in Jamestown in 1642. A member of the gentry, he soon built a large house on over 2,000 acres near Jamestown. Here he raised fruit, rice, flax, and other plants, all of which he sold for profit.

As governor, Berkeley had to try to get along with three of England's rulers, as well as with his fellow Virginians. His disagreements with Nathaniel Bacon, a plantation owner, forced Berkeley from office. Although Berkeley was a firm believer in the future of Virginia, King Charles II called him back to England. He sailed to England in 1677, a discouraged man. He died later that year.

BACON'S REBELLION

Nathaniel Bacon was a young man from a wealthy family. He was the owner of a large plantation in the western part of the Virginia Colony. He was also elected to the House of Burgesses, and he led the life of a wealthy planter.

When Indians attacked a man who worked for him, Bacon's life changed. Bacon grew angry at Governor Berkeley's policies. People needed the western land, and they needed to be able to protect it. Bacon raised an army to fight the Indians.

Both the rich planters and the poor farmers in the western part of the colony backed Nathaniel Bacon. In 1676, Bacon's soldiers attacked and killed hundreds of Indians. Then Bacon and his men marched on Jamestown and burned it.

Bacon's Rebellion was the largest uprising in colonial America. It did not last long. Bacon died suddenly, and the rebellion was over. England's king was alarmed by the revolt. He called Governor Berkeley back to England, and Berkeley lost his job.

Voices from America

"He has raised unjust taxes. He has failed to protect us. He has, with a few favorites, run the colony and ignored the interests of the people. For these and other offenses we accuse Sir William Berkeley of treason."

—NATHANIEL BACON, 1676

A NEW CAPITAL

In 1699, Governor Francis Nicholson decided to move the capital of the Virginia Colony from Jamestown. Jamestown had always been a swampy, unhealthful place. He moved the capital to a town called Middle Plantation, six miles away.

Nicholson designed the town. He planned the streets and the places for stores and houses. He planted trees to give shade from the hot Virginia sun. The capitol building was at one end of town. The new College of William and Mary was at the other end.

It was a handsome town, but it needed a new name. Nicholson called it Williamsburg after England's King William. For most of the year, Williamsburg was a quiet college town. But when the House of Burgesses was in session, the town sprang to life. There were meetings, business dealings, parties, and excitement! In the 1700s, Williamsburg became a hotbed of new political thinking. Here a new idea of freedom took root far from England.

The Virginia capitol building in Colonial Williamsburg

THE IMPORTANCE OF VIRGINIA

The Virginia Colony is important in United States' history. For one thing, it was the first community of English settlers that survived. These settlers experienced many hardships. In spite of them, the settlers stayed, and more came. The way of life these men and women brought with them helped to shape our American culture.

That way of life included having laws made by people who were elected. The Virginia Colony had the first representative assembly. Today our cities, states, and the nation are governed this way.

The diseases and warfare of the Virginia Colony killed almost all of the Native Americans who lived in the region. This tragedy is one of the bad parts of Virginia's history.

Slavery is another dark part of this history, but those who came in chains helped to build America. African-American culture began in the Virginia Colony.

Finally, the leaders of the Virginia Colony were also leaders in the American Revolution. Some, like George Washington, Thomas Jefferson, and James Madison, became presidents. These former colonists helped to give birth to our nation.

Patrick Henry, a Virginia colonist, speaks out against English rule.

assembly a gathering of people; a group of lawmakers

charter a permit issued by a ruler or other authority to a colony. It states how the colony is to be organized and governed.

civilization an advanced way of life; highly developed and organized society

colony a settlement of people who leave one country to live in another

descendant an offspring; child, grandchild, great-grandchild, and so on

gentry landowners of high social position

hostage a person held by an enemy to insure that certain agreements will be carried out

indentured servant a person who is legally required to work for someone for a certain number of years. Settlers who could not pay for their trip to America were often indentured in exchange for payment of their fare.

invaders people who enter and take possession of a place

investors people who put money into something they hope will increase in value

legislature a group of people who make laws for a state or country

marshy like soft, wet land

massacre an especially cruel killing of many people

militia an army of citizens who are trained to defend a colony, town, or state

plantation a large farm on which such crops as cotton or tobacco are grown

veto the right of a governor or president to reject bills passed by a lawmaking body

warrior a person experienced in fighting battles

Index